PHOTOGRAPHY   Miles Cowsill
  Vicky Harrop

TEXT   Stan Basnett

EDITOR   Trevor Barrett

DESIGN   Tracey Harding

PUBLISHER   Lily Publications Ltd

ISBN   978 1 899602 58 2

Lily Publications
LIMITED

PO Box 33 Ramsey Isle of Man IM99 4LP
TEL 01624 898446
EMAIL lilypubs@manx.net
WEB www.lilypublications.co.uk
© 2008 Lily Publications Ltd

ACKNOWLEDGEMENTS

Lily Publications thank the following for their assistance with this title: Carol Basnett, Dave Collister, Double Red and Jo Clark.

◀ WEST: the common which edges the plantation in GLEN RUSHEN, inland from Niarbyl Bay.

Clerical Medical, part of the HBOS Group, is one of the Island's leading Offshore Life Companies and is delighted and proud to sponsor the Visions of Mann publication, having been in operation in the Isle of Man for over twenty-one years.

This beautiful book captures the essence of what the Isle of Man is all about whilst both promoting and protecting its unique identity and heritage.

Clerical Medical, in turn, relates to the Island's unique spirit and approach and has a strong people culture, employing a workforce of over 150. Clerical Medical works very closely with the Isle of Man Government, promoting the Island all over the world, and was appointed a Freedom to Flourish Champion in 2007.

The company has an outstanding record for employee retention and service and is firmly perceived as an integral part of a strong and supportive community. As a Freedom to Flourish Champion we believe wholeheartedly that this is a land of possibility, where everyone is encouraged to fulfil their potential, whatever that might be.

CMI Insurance Company Limited
Clerical Medical House Victoria Road Douglas Isle of Man IM99 1LT
TEL +44 (0) 1624 638888 FAX +44 (0) 1624 625900
WEB www.offshore.clericalmedical.com

Isle of Man
Giving you Freedom to Flourish

.........Then rises like a vision sparkling bright in nature's glee,

My own dear Ellan Vannin with its green hills by the sea..........

So say the words of one of the Isle of Man's best-loved national songs, and in doing so encapsulate with beautiful simplicity the theme and purpose of this book: to bring you eye-opening images alongside a lightning tour of the life and times of this extraordinary rock in the Irish Sea.

NORTH-EAST: between the high ground of North Barrule and the coast at Port Cornaa lies the Neolithic burial ▲ chamber of CASHTAL YN ARD, about 4,000 years old.

WEST: looking north from the slopes of CRONK NY ARREY LAA, which are rich in ancient sites, you can ▶ see why the reef which encloses the bay at Niarbyl (meaning 'the tail') is so called.

A FEW SNAPS FROM HISTORY

The most recent expert research and opinion puts the earliest known human inhabitants on the Isle of Man about 9,000 years ago, and a chequered evolution since has seen the comings and goings of a pretty eclectic mix – pagans to Celts to Christians to Vikings to an amalgam of people from adjacent islands.

During Norse (Viking) rule the island was first divided into six sheadings, a system still surviving for administrative purposes, and later into seventeen parishes. Each had its parish church, often built on or near the site of a keeill – a primitive form of church.

The Vikings also built a number of timber forts, the locations of two of which are today marked by the ruins of Peel Castle and the totally contrasting structure of magnificent Castle Rushen. Both date from the 13th century but did not attain their final proportions until the 14th century. Built of sandstone, Peel Castle has suffered the ravages of wind, rain and sea due to its exposed position. Limestone Castle Rushen has endured the passage of time with distinction, and is not only one of the best-preserved medieval castles in the British Isles but has also remained in use to the present day. Other, and lesser, defences were built by the Duke of Athol to fend off Cromwell, and some of these also survive.

◄ SOUTH: Castletown's medieval CASTLE RUSHEN is a rarity which defies its age. Visitors speak highly of it – but not necessarily from the Speaker's Garden, the entrance to which is shown here.

Through centuries of turbulence and power struggles, the Manx people emerged with a spirit of fierce independence, which was just as well because before 1900 life was hard. Most of the population survived through subsistence crofting (small-scale farming) and fishing. The fishing ports of Douglas, Ramsey, Castletown, Port St Mary and Peel developed the idea of building their own boats, and some of these yards went on to construct significant topsail schooners that travelled between the island, the Baltic and beyond. *Star of India*, built in 1863 in Ramsey and then named *Euterpe* (the muse of lyric poetry and music in Greek mythology), is now the oldest surviving full-rigged ship and is berthed at San Diego in the USA.

A much bigger picture of Isle of Man history is painted in captivating style by Manx National Heritage, which as well as managing the Manx Museum in Douglas presents numerous fascinating sites linked by the umbrella theme *The Story of Mann*. The ideal way to follow the plot is to start with the museum's video introduction and then hit the heritage trail around the island.

WEST: as sunset approaches, northern Ireland's MOUNTAINS OF MOURNE can look deceptively close. ▶

■ EAST: the exterior and interior of the Manx parliament's TYNWALD CHAMBERS in Douglas. This is where the House of Keys and the Legislative Council sit together as Tynwald Court to pass the island's laws. The building dates from 1894, prior to which Tynwald sat in Castle Rushen. The horned snuff box stands on the Speaker's desk in the House of Keys chamber.

THE SPIRIT OF INDEPENDENCE

The Manx are very proud of the fact that the Isle of Man has its own parliament, Tynwald, which was originated by the Vikings way back in 797 AD. The popularised image of the pagan Norsemen being little more than savage warriors whose sole aims in life were invasion, rape, pillage and plunder doesn't really fit the picture suggested by Manx history and experience, the Vikings obviously deciding that there was something about this island in the Irish Sea which compelled them to not only stay but to take charge, integrate with the locals and, eventually, convert to Christianity.

The form of government they introduced has evolved into the present-day Tynwald, which in 1980 became a ministerial system comprising twenty-four elected members of the House of Keys. The Legislative Council remains the upper house but elected from within the Keys, and the Bishop and Attorney General are now non-voting members.

A new position of President of Tynwald was also incorporated, stripping the Lieutenant Governor of any political role within government. Traditionally, the Lieutenant Governor – the British Crown's island representative – wielded considerable power and influence and was referred to as 'the Governor'.

■ **NORTH-EAST:** the mudflats at **RAMSEY** mark where the Sulby river once flowed to the sea, but in the early 19th century it was diverted after its original outlet silted up.

The Isle of Man remains a Crown dependency, whose titular head is Queen Elizabeth II, and although not a member of the European Community the island is a signatory to Protocol Three of the Treaty of Accession and thereby enjoys some of the benefits of membership. To the Manx people, the most useful and practical of these is probably that a Manx passport is also an EU passport. And although the Isle of Man receives no European development grants, it is free of the burden of ever having to pay any back.

No, no!

Only to go,

To flow,

To fling my spray in the sunny glow.

To splash,

To dash,

Heels over head with a crazy crash.

From HOM-VEG AND BALLURE'S RIVER by T E Brown

RICHES UNDERGROUND

It's hard to imagine a greater contrast in human occupations than monks bound by vows of poverty and miners risking life and limb to deprive the earth of its mineral riches. Yet early in the 13th century the enterprising monks of Rushen Abbey, at Ballasalla, began extracting deposits of lead and copper from the Manx landscape.

The Stanleys (Lords of Mann in the 18th century) also mined for lead and silver, but it wasn't until the 19th century that the full potential of the island's mineral wealth was realised and extensive mining brought new industry to the Foxdale area and Laxey. The hard rock mines were deep and costly to sink but the rewards were great, Laxey's production making it the wealthiest mine in the British Isles. By 1930 it had all ground to a halt, but Laxey's giant *Lady Isabella* waterwheel is a permanent reminder and a major visitor attraction in this particular chapter of *The Story of Mann*.

▲ NORTH-EAST: the area around RAMSEY HARBOUR was once a thriving centre of boatbuilding and associated trades.

◀ NORTH: in fact, the distinctive NORTHERN PLAIN – a mostly flat lowland area which spreads north and west of Ramsey (right of picture), the highest feature being the modest Bride Hills.

▲ WEST COAST: competitors in the annual Parish Walk – an 85-mile trek through the island's 17 parishes – seen here rising to the challenge of the Sloc, near Cronk ny Arrey Laa.

RICHES UNDER SAIL

A seafaring island nation without smuggling is like a pirate without a parrot – phoney and unimaginable.

During the early part of the 18th century, an influx to the island of wealthy merchants and others from England created an opportunity for avoiding payment of excessive taxes. In league with the indigenous population, they took advantage of their unique situation to cash in on a trade in wines, spirits and silks, smuggled into England from the Isle of Man, much to the chagrin of the Revenue men.

Fortunes were made and lost throughout this colourful period of the island's history. Eventually, and inevitably, it came to an end under the Revesting Act of 1765 when the Lordship of Mann reverted to the Crown. 'The trade' (as the illicit activity was known) was largely responsible for the early development of Douglas and its harbour.

EAST: The reds and golds of autumn, ST JOHN'S. ▶

WEST: the ceremonial face of ▶ TYNWALD DAY, hosted annually in the village of St John's in early July (usually 5th). It is a celebration of Manx national identity and independence, presided over on occasion by Lord of Mann – Her Majesty the Queen. Here, in 2008, she was represented by guest of honour Her Royal Highness the Princess Royal.

An important tradition is the reading out, in Manx Gaelic and English, of the new laws passed within the legislative year. Another is all the fun of the fair which entertains the crowds of locals and summer visitors when the pomp and ceremony are over.

THE GEOLOGISTS TELL US THAT...

The Isle of Man was formed by the uplifting of Cambrian slates, similar to those found in Wales and Cumbria. Features include granite intrusions, limestone and sandstone outcrops, and an area of extinct volcanic activity with basalt remains. In the last ice age, the action of advancing and retreating ice sheets created the landscape's present rounded profile, but the coastline is the direct result of the ceaseless weathering process of the sea.

The island is just over 50 kilometres (31 miles) long by about 20 kilometres (12.5 miles) at its widest point. The northern plain is an alluvial deposit from the ice age and is broken only by a small range of hills in the parish of Bride. The centre of the island is dominated by rounded glacial mountains which can be divided into two regions – east and west. The highest are in the east and include North Barrule (565m). At 621m, Snaefell is the highest mountain of all and lies midway between North Barrule and Greeba (421m). In the west is a chain of hills extending from Slieau Curn (350m) in the north to Sartfell (440m) in the south, the latter overlooking the villages of Ballaugh and Kirk Michael.

SOUTH: under the fortress eye of mighty Castle Rushen, CASTLETOWN'S HARBOUR is a safe ▶ and popular haven for visiting pleasure craft. Another welcome retreat for weary sailors is the waterside Castle Arms (for many years known as the Glue Pot) – one of the island's oldest surviving pubs.

▲ As Manx as the three legs emblem itself, the famous CAT with no tail is prized around the world. The true breed has no tail stump either, and its stance is much more characteristic of a wild hare than a domesticated moggy.

Dividing the island is a central valley which extends between the ports of Douglas on the east coast and Peel on the west. To the south of the valley stand more hills, notably Slieau Whallian (333m), Lhiattee ny Beinee (301m) and South Barrule (483m).

The southern plain is not as flat as the northern plain and despite being more built up is the second largest agricultural area. In the southernmost part of the island the plain is broken by Mull Hill, effectively a peninsula terminated by cliffs dropping to the sea. And off the south-west tip of the Isle of Man is the Calf of Man – a small islet and bird sanctuary in the safekeeping of Manx National Heritage and in summer months accessible to the public by boat from Port St Mary and Port Erin.

EAST: an eminent Victorian lady still looked up to today with very high regard is LADY ISABELLA – Laxey's ▶ great wheel, designed by Robert Casement. From 1854 until the industry ceased in the late 1920s, the wheel pumped water from deep within the lead-rich mines. The turn it does now is as the centrepiece for the Mines Experience – part of Manx National Heritage's islandwide Story of Mann presentation.

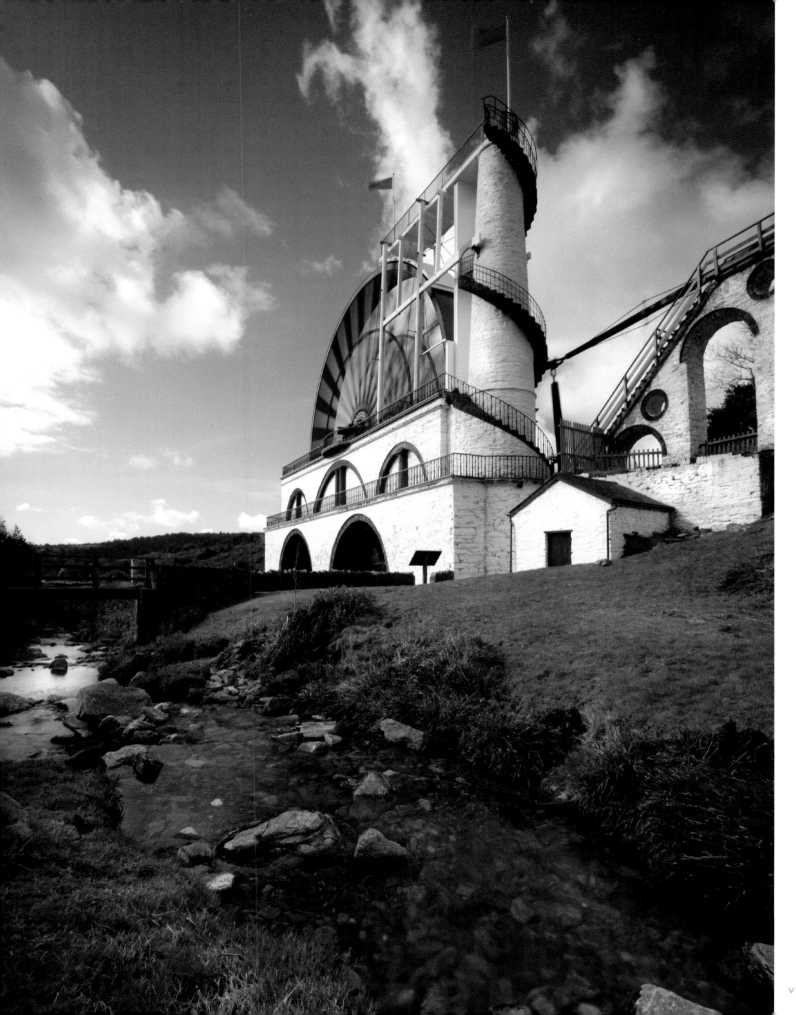

...BUT FOLKLORE SPINS A DIFFERENT YARN

Manx folklore is rich in myth, legend and superstition, and to many people is far more interesting and colourful than anything the geologists can ever hope to tell us.

According to its ancient tradition, the Isle of Man came about as a result of a battle between the mythical Irish giant Finn Mac Cuill and his sworn enemy, a Scottish giant. Mad Finn scooped up great clods of earth (in the process forming Lough Neagh and Loch Beg) and threw them at his fleeing opponent, but he was a lousy shot and the huge clods fell short and splashed into the Irish Sea, eventually becoming known as the Isle of Man and the Calf of Man.

Which of these origins is true? Take your choice!

▲ EAST: LADY OF MANN, one of the island's most popular car ferries, retired from Steam Packet service in 2005 and is seen here leaving Douglas harbour on her farewell crossing.

◄ EAST: VINTAGE TRANSPORT is one of the Isle of Man's very special attractions – and none more than the island's Victorian steam railway, still going strong after more than a century. Locomotive No 4, named *Loch* after a former Governor of the island, departs the station at Douglas bound for Port Erin, the line's southern terminus.

"THE TOURISTS ARE COMING!"

This was the shout which welcomed the predilection of the Victorians and Edwardians to take the waters. The holiday industry arrived on the Isle of Man as the working classes, with money in their pockets courtesy of the Industrial Revolution, discovered that this gem in the Irish Sea was very kindly positioned within easy reach of Scotland, Ireland and most importantly the north of England. It was an exciting time for all.

The introduction of steam propulsion led to the expansion of numerous shipping companies vying for the lucrative business. One was the Isle of Man Steam Packet Company, formed in 1830 by local businessmen keen to exploit the fact that the service from Liverpool and other northern ports was not up to requirements. Did they succeed? Put it this way: the Steam Packet is still going strong today.

Steam also made its presence felt on dry land as the island's huge upturn in wealth created a steam railway in 1873. It ran from Douglas to Peel and later to Port Erin and Ramsey. By 1876 Douglas had a horse tramway serving the promenade. In 1893 an electric tramway was built to Laxey and extended to Ramsey shortly after. Two years later an electric tramway was built from Laxey to the top of Snaefell. It was all go – and most of this Victorian transport still exists today, although the steam railway is in truncated form.

EAST: the old and the new. The Italianate style of the headquarters of the ISLE OF MAN BANK on the corner ▶ of Athol Street in Douglas reflects some of the old wealth that originated during the island's period of rapid growth as a popular holiday destination.

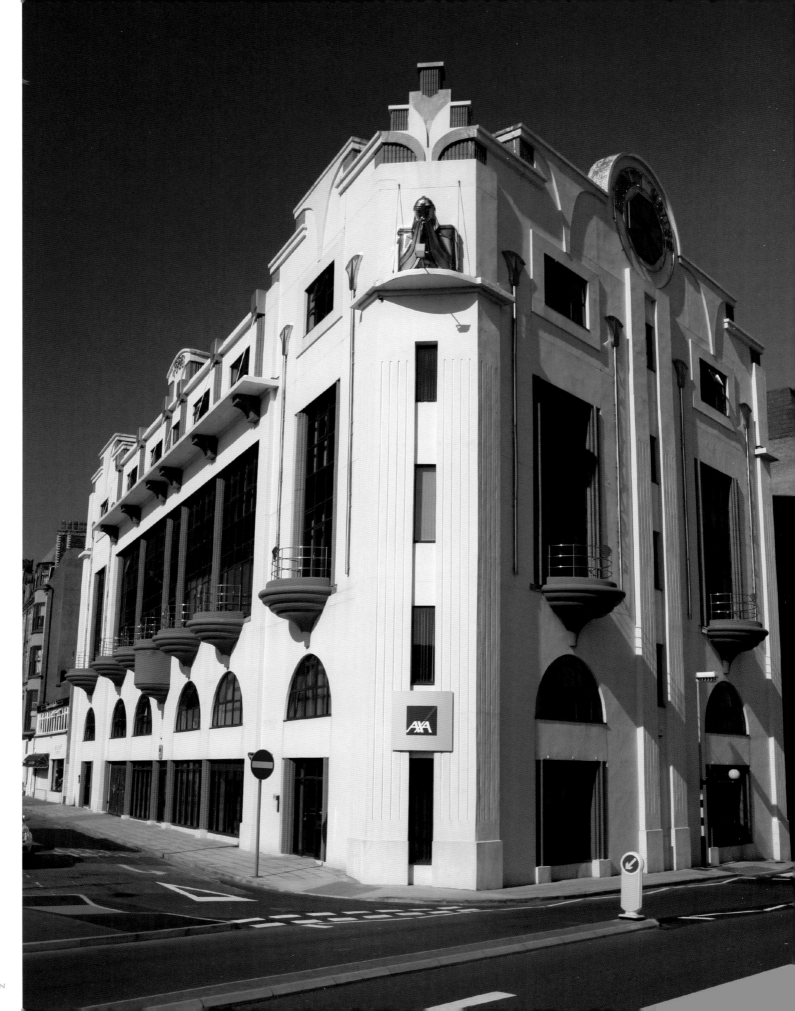

Other schemes which succeeded in getting off the ground but haven't endured included a cable tramway serving the steep streets of upper Douglas and a tramway along Marine Drive to Port Soderick. Nevertheless, the island was very well served by public transport and travel times to explore this intriguing holiday destination were dramatically reduced, putting many of the must-see places within much easier reach of Douglas and other towns.

The island went through an unprecedented period of development as towns and villages expanded to meet the demand for holiday accommodation. As the capital, Douglas naturally saw the greatest growth. Rows of boarding houses radiated from the lower part of the town, and a splendid promenade with a beautiful façade was built, eventually stretching across the whole bay.

Could there be a downside to all this new-found fame and fortune? Unfortunately, yes. Dependency on a seasonal market, with its natural fluctuations and unpredictable factors such as weather, led to a boom-and-bust type of economy. But still the island prospered.

Then two world wars came along and disrupted this business, which never really recovered from the effects of the second conflict. But the real blow was delivered by the advent of cheap package holidays to sunnier climes in the 1950s – a development which affected not only the Isle of Man but all traditional seaside resorts around Britain. Suddenly, people had discovered another world out there. It was called the Mediterranean.

◀ The new AXA building, on the corner of Walpole Avenue and Bath Place, stands on the site once occupied by the Royalty Cinema.

■ EAST: a sure sign of growing affluence – the old inner harbour at DOUGLAS transformed into a multi-pontoon marina for pleasure boats.

".... I do swear that I will without respect of favour or friendship, love or gain, consanguinity or affinity, envy or malice, execute the Laws of this Isle justly, betwixt our Sovereign Lady the Queen and her subjects within this Isle and betwixt Party and Party as indifferently as the herring backbone doth lie in the midst of the fish."

An extract from the OATH OF THE DEEMSTER

■ EAST: the COURTHOUSE in Douglas and the contemporary herring sculpture – symbolic of the island's legal system.

Isle of Man winters subsequently brought with them the icy chill of major unemployment. The Manx government answered it in part with road improvement schemes providing winter season work, but men left the island in significant numbers to earn their daily bread elsewhere – often in south-east England's sugar beet industry or in Ireland, digging peat.

Many Manx traditional boarding houses were gradually converted into flats. Hotels closed and fell into disrepair through lack of maintenance. Fishing and farming, which had blossomed with tourism, were badly affected too.

One notable survivor through all this turmoil was TT racing, introduced in 1907. And although Manx tourism in the 21st century looks very different from those early halcyon days, the TT still attracts massive crowds during festival fortnight and the lap record for the famous 37.73-mile Mountain Course now stands, incredibly, at a little over 130 mph – a fantastic speed given that the event is contested on ordinary public roads which in many places are narrow, twisty and hazardous, and everywhere challenging.

EAST: getting all steamed up in the shoe shop – the HORSETRAM FARRIER at work. ▶
Plus more views of Douglas, including the TOWER OF REFUGE – built for sailors shipwrecked on the treacherous Conister Rock reef which lies in wait perilously close to the harbour.

■ The **TT FESTIVAL** draws crowds of enthusiasts from all over the world to see this legendary road racing event, which celebrated its centenary in 2007. These pictures capture the true spirit and fervour of road racing.

▼ Crowds are rarely this big in practice week, seen here watching sidecars from the enclosure overlooking **BRADDAN BRIDGE**.

▲ Waiting for the flag to drop at St John's for the **2007 RE-ENACTMENT** of the first (1907) **TT**. The startline official in Edwardian garb is Tony East, owner of the ARE Collection in Kirk Michael and one of the prime movers behind this successful event.

◀ Old hands in close company. **IAN LOUGHER** (Stobart Honda 7) leads **ADRIAN ARCHIBALD** (TAS Suzuki 2), who started 50 seconds before him. They finished fifth and seventh respectively.

▼ All three wheels off the road as **DAVE MOLYNEUX** and **RICK LONG** power their way to victory. ▼ **ROD GOULD**, 1970 250cc world champion, prepares to take off in the 2007 Parade of Champions.

The TT spectacle pulls in a global audience as the island is transformed by rallies, rideouts, rock concerts, fun fairs, fireworks and an invasion of motor bikes of every conceivable make and colour. The atmosphere is electric and the chat and camaraderie give the island a unique cosmopolitan flavour. There is simply nothing else like the Isle of Man TT anywhere in the world.

▲ **JOHN MCGUINNESS** in the Senior TT.

▲ **JOHN MCGUINNESS** with his son, just after John completed his record-breaking 130mph lap.

The island's tourism industry today is focused on other speciality events too. Sport and competitive games feature prominently in the calendar, with festivals dedicated to rugby, football, walking, darts, chess, bowls and more, as well as other motor cycling and motorsport events such as off-road trials and rallying.

Popular activities regularly bring people across the Irish Sea to enjoy all sorts of activities – golf, diving, fishing, mountain biking, sailing, birdwatching, whale and dolphin watching, and a whole raft of watersports. There is plenty here for railway and transport enthusiasts, who are well catered for too with weekend and longer special events.

One of the most popular and recent innovations was the introduction in 2004 of the Isle of Man Walking Festival, which quickly developed into two annual festivals. There are many public rights of way, all well maintained and signposted, challenges varying between the extremes of the long-distance coastal path (Raad ny Foillan: road of the gull) and circular town trails and gentle strolls in any of the seventeen enchanting Manx national glens. It's an amazing diversity of options for one modest island – and wherever you go there's a change of scenery around every corner.

WEST: flashback to a quieter way of life. Church Lane, skirting the old church of St Peter's, is typical of the narrow ▶ streets and alleyways which even today are so characteristic of PEEL.

EAST: so many tall buildings fronting the sea mean that this could only be the sweeping crescent of DOUGLAS ▼ BAY, viewed here from Port Jack, at the Onchan (northern) end.

◄ EAST: the Isle of Man is a Crown dependency, the Queen (Lord of Mann) represented on the island by a Governor – a tradition which still endures. BEMAHAGUE HOUSE at Onchan is the Governor's official residence.

A LAND OF HIGH FINANCE AND LOW TAXATION

In the first instance, the Manx government responded to the challenges of changing fortunes by encouraging light industry. But the high costs of importing raw materials and then exporting finished products proved prohibitive, and in the 1970s the search for an alternative laid the foundations for establishing a finance industry.

Together with many associated activities, this has revolutionised the island's economy and the population has grown to around the 80,000 mark – its highest ever. The economy is buoyant, unemployment is at an all-time low and young people no longer have to leave the island in search of work. In fact, they command salaries the envy of their parents and beyond the belief of grandparents!

Douglas has seen a tremendous regeneration of old properties, many of which had reached the end of their useful life. A huge expansion of office development and new banking premises has changed the face of the business centre of the capital. The promenade too now boasts an attractive new façade, sympathetic apartment development replacing older run-down hotels and guesthouses yet retaining some of the Victorian splendour in their design.

In so many ways the Isle of Man is a picture – as the pages of this book will show you.

▲ EAST: DOUGLAS HARBOUR as seen from Douglas Head just as the Steam Packet's fastcraft VIKING is arriving.

LEFT TO RIGHT the departing BEN MY CHREE – the flagship of the Steam Packet; the statue of 19th-century Douglas resident SIR WILLIAM HILLARY, who in 1824 founded what became the Royal National Lifeboat Institution; DOUGLAS HEAD LIGHTHOUSE; and the popular Victorian attraction, now restored and reopened to visitors – the CAMERA OBSCURA.

▲ **EAST: DOUGLAS BAY** at Onchan Head, where (on the corner of Imperial Terrace and Hague Terrace) stands this statue of Scotsman Steve Hislop – a very popular TT champion (11 wins) who died tragically when his helicopter crashed in July 2003.

LEFT TO RIGHT The **TOWER OF REFUGE**, which was initiated by Sir William Hillary; a detail of the sculpture in the sunken gardens on Douglas promenade which depicts the rescue of survivors from the ship **ST GEORGE** (wrecked on Conister Rock in a gale in November 1830); the crest of **DOUGLAS HARBOUR COMMISSIONERS**; and an early-morning departure of the Steam Packet's **BEN MY CHREE**.

EAST: LEFT TO RIGHT the refurbished JUBILEE CLOCK, presented to Douglas in 1887 to mark the occasion of Queen Victoria's Jubilee, stands at the entrance to Victoria Street on the prom; a general view over DOUGLAS with the marina in the foreground and low tide in the bay; and the restaurant which was formerly Clinch's Brewery, located at the head of the marina.

EAST: the long pontoon gives access and security to the many boats which have transformed Douglas's old working inner harbour into a first-class modern MARINA. ▶

■ EAST: "Presenting, for your delight and entertainment, the famous, the fabulous, the revered, the restored – Frank Matcham's magnificent GAIETY THEATRE and Opera House!"

It took more than 10 years, and a great deal of dedication, fundraising and detective work, to return this wonderful but sadly run-down theatre to as near to its original 1900 condition as was possible (given the constraints of today's health and safety and other regulations). The result has put it amongst the world's finest surviving theatres built during the heyday of the Victorian and Edwardian era – and particularly those designed by the eminent Matcham. The remarkable and often very funny story of the restoration and how it came about is told in Lily Publications' *Saving the Gaiety*.

■ EAST: although it occupies the site of its long-forgotten and outdated predecessor of the same name, the new multi-million-pounds VILLA MARINA can justifiably be called new in every sense – an excellent venue combining first-class entertainment staged in the Royal Hall with excellent hospitality, beautiful grounds and gardens, and an invigorating seafront location on Douglas promenade. Rock concerts, dance competitions, festivals, lavish celebrations, conferences: Ivy Benson, Joe Loss and other old-time Villa Marina megastars would most definitely approve!

▼ EAST: the pleasures of the prom. DOUGLAS seafront is not only wide, spacious and inviting; it is also 2 miles long – an ideal place for a relaxing stroll, invigorating walk or breathtaking bike ride.

▼ **EAST:** the great variety of church buildings and architecture is a notable feature of the Isle of Man. For example, in Onchan **ST PETER'S CHURCH HALL** of 1898 was designed by Baillie Scott.

▲ **EAST: ST GEORGE'S**, the oldest surviving church in Douglas, built in 1871 and in recent years enhanced by the installation of the peal of bells.

◄ **EAST: OLD KIRK BRADDAN**, originally the parish church for part of lower Douglas, was built in its present form in 1773. The graveyard is even older, its headstones recording a wealth of local history.

▲ **EAST:** power to the people. Douglas's new **POWER STATION** has the capacity to supply virtually the total needs of the island.

▲ **EAST:** the **MILLENNIUM OAKWOOD** was established to celebrate the beginning of the 21st century. On 9th March 2000, a total of 6,754 trees were planted – one by every primary school child on the Isle of Man.

▲ **EAST:** standing on the outskirts of Douglas is the new **NOBLE'S HOSPITAL** – the third since 1888 to bear the name of Henry Bloom Noble, the island's greatest benefactor, whose home at one time was the original Villa Marina.

■ **EAST: GROUDLE GLEN**, just north of Douglas and accessible from the capital via the **MANX ELECTRIC RAILWAY**, was popular with Victorian holidaymakers. Attractions included a sea lion and polar bear compound, served by a **NARROW-GAUGE RAILWAY**. The animals have long since departed but the railway survives, restored by enthusiasts and operated by them at various times during summer and other holidays.

The **WATERWHEEL** and wheelhouse, dating from the 1890s, which powered Groudle Glen's fairy lights. ▷

◄ **EAST: OLD KIRK LONAN CHURCH** has its origins in the 12th century and although still in use on special occasions has been replaced by the 'new' parish church, built in 1733.

▼ **EAST:** standing in the graveyard of the original old church is the beautiful **LONAN STONE** – a wheel-headed cross, Celtic in style and dating from the 9th or 10th century.

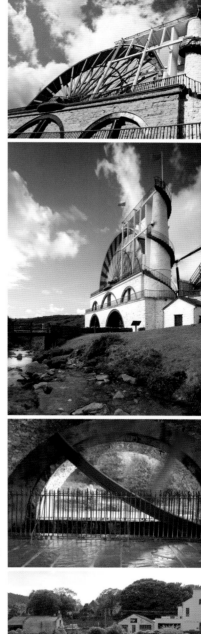

Laxey was a mining village many years ago,

There were six hundred miners working under Captain Rowe,

But the bottom of the mineshaft was below the waterline

So the owners built a wheel to pump the water from the mine.

And the Laxey Wheel keeps turning, turning, turning

In the Lady Iasabella's memory

And while the water flows the Laxey Wheel still goes

And the Laxey River runs down to the sea.

LAXEY WHEEL by Stuart Slack

■ EAST: Stuart Slack's song tells the story of the Great Laxey Wheel's purpose in life, but today Laxey has two wheels – LADY ISABELLA of the song and LADY EVELYN, which served the Snaefell mine further up the valley and is now restored and displayed on Laxey's old washing floors (where the mined ore was cleaned to be sold).

▲ EAST: from Douglas you can reach Laxey by either of two very leisurely routes – pleasure boat or Manx Electric Railway. Laxey attractions include riding the restored Mines Railway and seeing how Manx tartan is woven at St George's woollen mills.

LAXEY BEACH and GARWICK BAY ▶

▼ EAST: lovely LAXEY and its beautiful bay.

▲ **EAST:** lying in a deep ravine less than two miles north of Laxey, and famed for its spectacular waterfall, is **DHOON GLEN** – reputedly haunted by the ghost of a girl who drowned in the pool. The photographs alongside show TOP TO BOTTOM the burial site which has the misnomer **KING ORRY'S GRAVE**; **DHOON HALT** on the Manx Electric Railway, giving access to the glen; the beach estuary and the valley of the **CORNAA RIVER**, which flows through Ballaglass Glen on its route to the sea; and **BALLAJORA** – another 'station' on the Manx Electric Railway, north-east of the glen and near Maughold Head.

◀ In this same north-eastern corner of the Isle of Man, in the parish of Maughold, is beautiful, peaceful **BALLAGLASS GLEN** – a big attraction to artists, photographers and walkers, and renowned for its spring bluebells. The Manx Electric Railway delivers you to the glen's top entrance.

We went to climb Barrule
Wind light, air cool —
But when we reached the crest
That fronts Cornaa
A black cloud leaned its breast
Upon the bay —

From MARY QUAYLE: THE CURATE'S STORY
by T E Brown

NORTH-EAST: if you love the countryside and the freedom of exploring wide ▶
open spaces on foot, all you have to know is that these views are further evidence
of the great natural beauty and scenic variety to be enjoyed in the parish of
MAUGHOLD.

■ **NORTH-EAST:** although in its present form **MAUGHOLD CHURCH** dates from 1901, it is one of the oldest churches on the island. Its origins are 12th-century and some of the surviving structure goes back to 1275. And as well as being in a spectacular coastal location near the headland and lighthouse, both church and churchyard are guardians of priceless historic treasures, including many ancient crosses preserved under cover and the 14th-century Maughold pillar cross, featuring one of the earliest known carvings of the Three Legs of Man.

T'was once I loved a lass, I swore I loved her true

And that I did so long as we held Ramsey still in view,

And that I did so long as we held Ramsey still in view.

Ramsey Town, O Ramsey Town, Shining by the sea!

Here's a health to my true love, where-so-e'er she be!

MANX NATIONAL SONG BOOK: from RAMSEY TOWN by E Crabb

■ NORTH: in the foreground is the small seaside hamlet of **PORT E VULLEN** (meaning port of the mill) and beyond is Ramsey and the wide sweep of Ramsey Bay.

■ **NORTH:** the lighthouse, one of two on the twin north and south piers, helps mark the entrance to RAMSEY'S busy harbour, which is still commercially active. The harbour's most easily-recognised feature is the 1892 iron swingbridge – 225 feet (68.5 m) in length.

◄ QUEEN'S PIER at Ramsey, built in 1886, stretched 2,300 feet (700 m) into the sea and carried a tramway, enabling ships to land at low tide. The pier is not only long disused but also faces an uncertain future.

■ NORTH: at SHELLAG POINT, about midway between Ramsey and the northernmost Point of Ayre, the low Bride Hills touch the wild, exposed coastline and are subject to continuous erosion by the relentless action of the sea.

84 VISIONS OF MANN

On the Kirk Bride road there's a path you'll see
Betwix' the brews that the sheep have wore
And a cart-track leadin' to the shore;
And a pleasant little place they're callin' –
What's this it is now? – aye, "The Vollin"

TOMMY BIG EYES by T E Brown

■ NORTH: built in 1818 and standing on steep shingle banks, **POINT OF AYRE LIGHTHOUSE** warns of a notoriously treacherous stretch of deep water close to shore which is agitated by powerful conflicting currents. In 1890 a smaller supporting light was erected, known to mariners as Winkie because of its quick flashing signal.

NORTH: the gently rolling fields and pastureland of the **BRIDE HILLS** and northern plain. ▶

Westward to Jurby, eastward if you look,

The coast runs level to the Point of Ayre.

A waste of sand, sea holly, and wild thyme – wild thyme and bent. The Mull of Galloway is opposite.

Adown the farthest west,

Not visible now, lie stretched the hills of Morne.   From BELLA GORRY: THE PAZON'S STORY by T E Brown

■ **NORTH-WEST:** in prehistoric times, large areas of the flat northern plain were covered by shallow lakes, and only centuries of drainage have enabled successful cultivation of the land to transform it into one of the island's most fertile regions. An important drainage channel in this process has been the 17th-century **LHEN TRENCH**, viewed here looking towards the Guilcagh from the Rhendhoo Road, close to Jurby East. Remnants of some lakes still remain, an example being the dub (pond) at Glascoe in Bride.

NORTH-WEST: for centuries **BISHOPSCOURT**, at Ballaugh, was the ▶
official home of successive Bishops of Man. Today it is a private residence.

The photographs below show **KIRK MICHAEL** parish church, dating from ▼
1835; **JURBY** parish church – adopted by RAF Jurby during the Second
World War – which was built in 1829 and perches precariously on Jurby Head;
the **SULBY GLEN HOTEL**; and the old parish church of **ST MARY DE
BALLAUGH**, dating in its present form from 1717 and noted for its leaning
gate pillars.

■ WEST: (left to right) the coast south of JURBY HEAD ends in sand cliffs exposed to constant weathering from wind and sea, particularly near the village of Kirk Michael; the view looking north from CASS STRUAN, the nature of the coast changing to sandstone nearer to Peel; the western hills as seen from the hamlet of CRONK Y VODDY, just north of Glen Helen.

The Sherragh Vane
Is up Sulby glen,
High up, my men –
High up – you'll not see a sight of it
From the road at all,
By rayson of the height of it –

From KITTY OF THE SHERRAGH VANE by T E Brown

▼ **WEST (CENTRAL):** carved by the Sulby River – the longest on the Isle of Man – **SULBY GLEN** is still deliciously wild and unspoiled. The smaller pictures (both pages) show Sulby's annual Royal Manx Agricultural Show.

The snow's on the mountains, the snow's in the gill;
My sheep they have wander'd all over the hill;
Uprise then my shepherds with haste let us go
Where my sheep are all buried deep under the snow.

SHEEP UNDER THE SNOW by W H Gill

▲ NORTH (CENTRAL): from Laxey, the SNAEFELL MOUNTAIN RAILWAY takes you to the top of the island's highest peak, 2,036 feet (621 m) above sea level, with many interesting views along the 5-mile route.

◄ SNAEFELL viewed from the slopes of Beinn y Phott.

▼ CENTRAL: ST LUKE'S CHURCH, a chapel of ease, stands between the rivers Glass and Baldwin just south of Injebreck Reservoir and dates back to 1836.

◄ CENTRAL: INJEBRECK RESERVOIR, in the West Baldwin valley in the middle of the island, has served Douglas since coming on stream in 1905. It also provides recreation for local yacht clubs and is a haven for walkers and wildlife.

▲ **WEST:** imposing St Patrick's Isle, with its impressive medieval curtain walls enclosing the ruins of **PEEL CASTLE** and St German's Cathedral, 'guards' the entrance to Peel harbour – a task for which it was obviously well equipped in centuries past. In 1884 a new church named St German was completed in the town, consecrated in 1980 as the new Peel Cathedral and reinstating the modest fishing port's claim to city status!

▲ **WEST:** the Isle of Man's legendary ancient sea god and shape-shifting magician Manannan Mac Lir has a strong presence in this coastal view over **PEEL** looking north. His protective cloak of mist shrouds the hills, and the House of Manannan heritage centre stands along the waterfront seen in the right foreground.

◄ The colourful narrow streets of **PEEL** are full of character and interest. Catching the eye beyond the rooftops in the centre of the picture is the castle's distinctive 11th-century Round Tower on St Patrick's Isle.

Hear us, O Lord, from Heav'n thy dwelling place.

Like them of old, in vain we toil all night .....

Unless with us thou go, who art the light;

Come, then, O Lord, that we may see thy face.

MANX NATIONAL SONG BOOK W H Gill

▲ WEST: when the Irish Sea throws a tantrum, the old fishing port's harbour and promenade catch quite a battering.

Calm again. The white building beyond the boats is HOUSE OF MANANNAN – the Manx National Heritage attraction which ▶ reveals much about Peel and St Patrick's Isle and their place in the island's history.

▲ WEST: on top of CORRIN'S HILL is the square tower built in 1806 by a staunch non-conformist named Corrin. It is said that he, his wife and child are buried in the unconsecrated ground nearby. The tower is known as Corrin's Folly.

◄ This church tower, along with the building's outer walls, are all that now remain of ST PETER'S in Peel's Market Place, the remainder having been demolished in 1958.
The smaller pictures show various aspects of Peel life, including the interior of the present-day cathedral and hardy souls enjoying the customary NEW YEAR'S DAY DIP.

◀ **WEST: PEEL'S** modern waterfront redevelopment of apartments and shops is in sharp contrast to the early 19th-century tower of St Peter's.

■ WEST: agriculture is no longer a major contributor to the Manx economy, but cereal production and management of the rural landscape are still very important to conserving Isle of Man identity, tradition and wildlife.

■ WEST: in Manx custom, midsummer's day was 5th July – a tradition still observed by the annual TYNWALD DAY ceremony and celebrations hosted at the village of St John's, five miles inland from Peel. These photographs of the 2008 event, presided over by Her Royal Highness the Princess Royal, show the pomp and colour of the occasion, including four-tiered Tynwald Hill – the focal point of the formal ceremony – and the Royal Chapel. The latter has served the community since 1849 and is an integral aspect of Tynwald Day.

▲ **CENTRAL:** this eye-opening panorama seen from the A24 Douglas to Foxdale road near the Braaid overlooking **GLEN VINE** (the community in the left foreground) is a variation on that which was captured so famously by artist and Manx resident John Martin (1789-1854) in his painting *Plains of Heaven*. This view shows the valley of West Baldwin beyond Glen Vine and the snow-dusted ridge of Snaefell in the middle distance.

■ **WEST:** the main picture shows the Rhenass river cutting a course through enchanting **GLEN HELEN** before joining the River Neb en route to St John's and the sea at Peel. The bridge is also a distinctive feature of this very popular glen. The village is **PATRICK**, just south of Peel on the A27 west coast road.

▲ WEST: sunset over the beautiful little coastal retreat and cottages of NIARBYL, which featured in the popular screen comedy *Waking Ned* and is a favoured location for the island's TV and film production industry. Below these two photographs is a view from the coastal footpath as it descends to Traie Vane south of Niarbyl.

Looking south along the coastal footpath from Corrin's Hill, Peel, towards NIARBYL. ▶

The view across BAIE MOOAR (the big bay) from Niarbyl to Cronk ny Arrey Laa. ▼

THE KING OF THE SEA

Over the Cronk ny Irree Laa
The sun's bright signal shines;
'Tis time to haul our glittering train
And ship our loaded lines.
Oh! the herring, boys, the herring,
Oh! the herring, boys, for me!
Red or kippered, fresh or pickled,
Oh! the herring is king of the sea!

From the MANX NATIONAL SONG BOOK: by J Fred Gill

◄ WEST: one of the island's most beautiful views – from the top of CRONK NY ARREY LAA (Hill of the Day Watch), looking south to the Mull peninsula and the islet Calf of Man beyond.

On the summit of CRONK NY ARREY LAA is the Millennium Stone, ▶ dedicated at dawn on 1st January 2000. It looks over the fishing grounds of the island's west coast and is appropriately inscribed with the words of the Manx Fisherman's Hymn.

▼ SOUTH-WEST: in this panorama, the distinctive landmark of Milner's Tower identifies BRADDA HEAD on the left, the depression right of centre marks Fleshwick Bay and the hills to the right (south of Cronk ny Arrey Laa) are the Carnanes, which display evidence of prehistoric dwellings. The photograph was taken from the Howe (an old Norse word meaning hill) which stands alongside the A31 road between Cregneash and Port St Mary.

Where fuchsias blow and curlews call
O'er hill and glen and waterfall
In lightsome wind or sudden squall;
There lies my heart.

Where heather, gorse and sombre pine,
Aglow like stained glass or old wine,
Lend glory to the stern coastline;
There lies my heart.

From northern Point to southern Sound,
From east to west, full circle round,
Wherein all things true manx are found;
There lies my heart.

And should perchance my simple song,
Portray there glories which for long
Have been our heritage – proud, strong;
How glad my heart!

WHERE FUCHSIAS BLOW by Kathleen Faragher

■ SOUTH-WEST: from the top down, five of these pictures are of **PORT ERIN** (the promenade, the bay, houses backing the prom, and the railway station exterior and very impressive interior), and the bottom photograph shows the foundations of prehistoric hut circles on the summit of Mull Hill above Port Erin bay.

▲ PORT ERIN, like Peel, is well versed in the art of putting on a show of truly spectacular sunsets.

 SOUTH-WEST: the two faces of PORT ERIN. The older buildings on the lower promenade are the remnants of the original fishing village, and the advent of the steam railway in 1894 led to Port Erin's growing popularity as a holiday destination and the subsequent development of the upper promenade with hotels and boarding houses.

■ SOUTH-WEST: looking across the SOUND to the main island from the CALF OF MAN – a small islet which is a bird and wildlife sanctuary and home to an important (ornithologically speaking) BRITISH BIRD OBSERVATORY. The ripping tidal currents and deep water of the Sound make this a particularly hazardous place for shipping – hence the proliferation of navigational aids. Shown in these photographs are THOUSLA BEACON (centre, main picture), the tall tower of solar-powered CHICKEN ROCK LIGHTHOUSE and a lighthouse on the Calf of Man (which has had three in its time). The Calf's farm buildings provide accommodation for the seasonal warden and visitors.

So we pulled uncommon hard till we got
To the Thoushla — bless me! That's the spot —
That's where ye gets the strength of the tide —
Aw, despard though! But slack inside,
And shelter from the sea, that's more;
So that's what we were making for.

From CHRISTMAS ROSE by T E Brown

▲ The **SOUTH-WESTERN CORNER** of the Isle of Man, on the Mull peninsula, is a wild and fascinating place.
As well as the man-made cafe, with its wonderful panoramic window looking out across the **SOUND** to the
Calf of Man, there are natural attractions such as seals basking on the rocks. The top photograph shows the
treacherous nature of the currents which race through the Sound – a narrow channel in which Kitterland, a small
islet, presents a further hazard to any boats daring to pass this way. The view below, also looking across to the
Calf, is as seen from a little further along the peninsula's southern coast, towards Spanish Head.

On the eastern side of the peninsula, not far beyond Spanish Head, are two very distinctive geological coastal ▶
features. One is the Chasms – gigantic vertical rifts in the cliffs, descending 200 feet into the sea – and the other
is the attendant offshore stack known as the **SUGAR LOAF** rock (Cashtal y Stackey in Manx, meaning castle
of the stacks), which is a breeding site for seabirds.

■ **SOUTH-WEST:** the Mull peninsula again, on the slopes above the Sound close to Mull Hill, with four photographs taken in the vicinity of **CREGNEASH** – the village of whitewashed thatched cottages which as well as being a living community is also preserved by Manx National Heritage as an authentic example of how Manx crofters worked and lived in the 19th century. This includes using traditional farming methods and equipment.

■ **SOUTH-WEST:** stained glass windows are an attractive feature of St Peter's, the church in the centre of **CREGNEASH** village.

■ **SOUTH-WEST:** just across the neck of the Mull peninsula from Port Erin (which is on the west side) is **PORT ST MARY** on the east side – a coastal village with a charm all its own, born out of fishing and boat building, and today a haven for local and visiting pleasure craft of all shapes and sizes. Many believe that the harbour is the ideal spot for a proposed new marina development. Then there are the attractions of Port St Mary's Chapel Bay – a sun trap with a beautiful sandy beach.

▲ SOUTH-EAST: CASTLETOWN as seen from the coastal path at nearby Scarlett – an area marked by past volcanic activity.

▼ SOUTH-EAST: CASTLETOWN BAY on a winter's day. Castletown was the island's capital until 1865, and the outer harbour was busy with commercial traffic as recently as the 1970s, since when it has gradually become another haven for pleasure craft.

▲ A view from CHAPEL HILL (an interesting archaeological site west of Castletown) towards Port Erin.

◄ CASTLETOWN'S OUTER HARBOUR is protected from the battering of south-westerly gales by a breakwater.

▲ **SOUTH-EAST:** aspects of **CASTLETOWN**, the former capital of the Isle of Man, including TOP FROM LEFT Castle Rushen's curious one-fingered clock, dating from 1597; the Old Grammar School, established in 1698; the embracing arms that promise safe harbour; architectural features of old Castletown's many interesting buildings; traditional shops in Malew Street; the Old House of Keys, which is now a **STORY OF MANN** attraction; and notorious Hango Hill, once a place of execution.

◄ Anyone arriving at Castletown by sea is welcomed by these glorious pepper-pot lights on the harbour piers.

◄ SOUTH-EAST: the unspoilt **LANGNESS PENINSUA** is a haven for birdlife and wildlife – and also the home of Castletown's championship links golf course. The lighthouse tells of much sadder stories, though – of shipwreck and disaster, the peninsula prior to the lighthouse's arrival in 1880 having been a maritime graveyard for unsuspecting vessels. All Isle of Man lighthouses are now fully automated and are controlled by the Northern Lighthouse Board, as are those in Scotland and the isles.

▼ SOUTH-EAST: other features and landmarks of the Langness peninsula include the HERRING TOWER – built in 1816 in an attempt to keep shipping away from the treacherous rocks – and ST MICHAEL'S ISLE, on which stand the remains of two interesting features: a circular fort built by the Derby family to protect Castletown from invasion during the Civil War, and the ruins of St Michael's Chapel, dating from the 12th century.

▲ North of the peninsula on the island's east coast – Cass-ny-Hawin headland, near Port Soldrick. It is also known as SANTON GORGE – the point where the Santan burn enters the sea through a spectacular gorge carved during the ice age by the meltwater from the retreating ice sheet. The river is now a trickle by comparison.

▲ **LANGNESS LIGHTHOUSE** on early-morning watch.

■ SOUTH-EAST: RONALDSWAY is the island's only commercial airport, owned and operated by the Manx government. It is a far cry from its origins as an airfield in 1933 and war-time development by the Admiralty as the naval land base *HMS Urley*. Ronaldsway's modern terminal is now the envy of many regional UK airports, and at the time of this book going to press (November 2008) a major runway extension was under construction.

■ **SOUTH-EAST: BALLASALLA**, north of Castletown and the airport, is popular for attractions such as those shown here.

▼ **MONKS BRIDGE**, a 14th-century packhorse bridge (one of only a few of its type surviving in the British Isles) crosses the Silverburn river and was built by the monks of nearby Rushen Abbey.

▲ The large mill at **BALLASALLA** has long been converted to apartments but its architecture displays indisputable proof of its original use.

SILVERDALE GLEN is a big hit with families and young ▶ children. In this view you can almost smell the wild garlic.

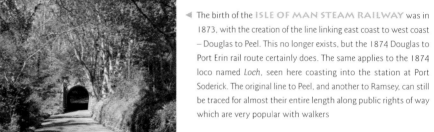

▲ **EAST:** a sea of bluebells near **SANTON** set the scene for this colourful view across country to the high ground of South Barrule in the west.

◀ The birth of the **ISLE OF MAN STEAM RAILWAY** was in 1873, with the creation of the line linking east coast to west coast – Douglas to Peel. This no longer exists, but the 1874 Douglas to Port Erin rail route certainly does. The same applies to the 1874 loco named *Loch*, seen here coasting into the station at Port Soderick. The original line to Peel, and another to Ramsey, can still be traced for almost their entire length along public rights of way which are very popular with walkers

▲ **EAST:** the automated lighthouse at **DOUGLAS HEAD** dates from 1892 – a replacement for one built sixty years earlier.

In recent decades **MARINE DRIVE** connected Douglas Head by road to Port ▷ Soderick, a small bay to the south much favoured by Victorian and Edwardian holidaymakers. But a landslide in 1977 has rendered it impassable to cars.

Now the beauty of the thing when childer plays is

The terrible wonderful length the days is.

Up you jumps and out in the sun

And you fancy the day will never be done;

And you're chasing' the bumbees hummin' so cross

In the hot sweet air among the goss,

Or gath'rin' blue-bells, or looking' for eggs,

Or peltin' the ducks with their yalla legs,

Or a climbin' and nearly breakin' your skulls,

Or a shoutin' for divilment after the gulls,

Or a thinkin' of nothin', but down at the tide

Singin' out for the happy you feel inside.

That's the way with the kids, you know,

And the years do come and the years do go,

And when you look back it's all like a puff,

Happy and over and short enough.

From BETSY LEE by T E Brown